INSIGHT OUT

WRITING FROM THE HEAD VOLUME II

This Edition Published by Headway Glasgow

In association with 'Writing From The Head'
(a group within Headway Glasgow)
260 Bath Street, Glasgow, G2 4JP
0141 332 8878 : info@headwayglasgow.org
www.headwayglasgow.org

Copyright 2015 © 2015 Writing From The Head

All authors maintain moral and legal rights to the undernoted works. No part of it may be reprinted or produced or utilised in any form or by electronic, mechanical or other means now known or hereafter invented, including photocopying and recording or in any information storage or retrieval system without permission in writing from the individual author and their right to be identified as the author being asserted. Permission to reproduce or reprint can be obtained directly with the author or through Headway Glasgow.

ISBN – PAPERBACK – 9780957469327

ISBN – E READER – 9780957469334

A CIP Catalogue record for this book is available
from the British Library.

Printed by Clydeside Press, 37 High Street, Glasgow.

Every effort has been made to contact copyright holders. However, the publisher will be glad to rectify, in future editions, any inadvertent omissions brought to their attention.

Cover Image: Lighthouse by Ricky Gordon- Headway Art Group

Acknowledgements

The editors would like to thank the following for making sure this book was produced.

All the authors who contributed their work.

The Headway Glasgow Staff for the tea, biscuits and support.
The Renfield Centre Staff for not chucking us out!
Tom Leonard and Robert Jeffrey for paying us a visit.
And all the others who helped us clear away the blocks to creativity.

'Writing From The Head' would like to thank our tutor Jonathan Anderson, for his patience and knowledge of our circumstances.

Edited by Jonathan Anderson.

This book was able to take shape and to be completed with the financial assistance of **Creative Scotland**.

Registered Charity Number SC030113

For more information about 'Writing from the Head', or to purchase further copies of this book, please contact -

Headway Glasgow,
260 Bath Street,
Glasgow, G2 4JP.

Website – www.headwayglasgow.org
Email – info@headwayglasgow.org

Telephone – 0141 332 8878

To allow Headway Glasgow to continue the work we have been doing with those affected by Acquired Brain Injury, donations can be made through our website using 'justgiving' or sent to the above address.

WHO WE ARE

'Writing From The Head' is a small group, consisting of people who have an Acquired Brain Injury, together with support staff. The group was formed within Headway Glasgow, a charity which works with people who have an Acquired Brain Injury. The function of the group is to encourage members to gain confidence through discussion and writing. Concentration, fatigue, being easily stressed and memory problems are just some of the issues to be faced on a daily basis. As a group we aim to help and encourage each other to be as creative as we can. Having no time limits and being surrounded by like minded people enables us to achieve this.

People who have contributed to this book include ...

Pamela Watt, Steven Walker, Innes Walker, Jim Vincent, Anne-Marie Ure, David Thomson, Neill Sloan, Mary Penny, Charlie McGoldrick, Lorraine Kennedy, Bob Gray, Mike Gallagher, Melissa Fairbanks, John Campbell, John Burns, Rosemary Boyle, Katya Bisset, Jonathan Anderson.

Dedicated to the memory of
Robert Fergusson

1750 – 1774

'rejoice, an' hail you wi a grateful voice'

"Edinburgh-born poet Robert Fergusson achieved so much poetical success in his short life of twenty-four years that Robert Burns called him 'my elder brother in the muse' when he commissioned a headstone in Canongate Churchyard, thirteen years after the poet had been buried there, a pauper in an unmarked grave.

Almost all of Fergusson's poems were produced in an extraordinary two years of production, heralded by the appearance of 'The Daft Days' in the *Weekly Magazine* in 1772, celebrating the New Year holidays in January with plenty of food, drink and mirth to set against a cold climate. Fergusson had struck a vein with his observations of his native city, not least in its festivals and seasonal occupations, so 'Hallow Fair' memorialises the annual fair held in November, with its stalls and tents, fortune-tellers and horse-dealers.

Nevertheless, by 1773, Fergusson's life was falling into disarray. Failing health and growing fears of death left him depressed and cost him his job. A serious head injury, perhaps incurred in a tumble downstairs, tipped him into increasingly violent and still more morbid fears. Towards the end of 1774 he was taken from his mother's house, against his will, and lodged in the Bedlam next to the Edinburgh poorhouse, where he died in a straw-littered cell within weeks. He was only 24."

Professor Roderick Watson,

the Scottish Poetry Library

scottishpoetrylibrary.org.uk

CONTENTS

When You Look At Me

When you look at me,
What exactly do you see?
I know you probably don't see the struggle,
My eyes tell a different story
but I hide it well when I clown around.

When you look at me,
What exactly do you see?
Do you even notice my brain injury?
Ask yourself this if I may,
What do you think I can do during my day?
I used to work two jobs, go to nursing school,
even squeezed in some summer fun
like concerts, whitewater rafting
and kayaking too.
Now I can't study, watch movies,
bike or anything like before.
After half a day, I'm so fatigued lately
I go home to my room and just shut the door.

When you look at me
what dynamic do you think I have for my family?
Mom, Dad, Brothers, Sisters?
Well my family is more like the resistors.
Due to my injury my family just didn't understand.
They decided for me, they had a different plan.

When you look at me,
Where do you think my home might be?
Just when I thought my life couldn't get any worse,
and I must be cursed.
When I got home one day,
all my things were put out to the porch and lawn,
the family I knew all my life was now long gone.
So now I sleep in a shelter, I'm homeless,
but just know, I'm ok, I'm never hopeless.

When you look at me,
don't feel sorry for these
struggles have strengthened me.
And yes, finally there is light in
the proverbial tunnel I now can see.

When you look at me,
what do you think my dream might be?
I have a new dream, a passion in my life.
It's to educate people about
our invisible struggle and fight.
So when you think of brain injury,
please don't think of just little old me.
There's so many of us with stories
that we are all willing to share,
so please join us, we'd love to see
others like yourself that truly care.

– Melissa Fairbanks

Ah Want Tae Be A Buddhist

Ah want tae be a Buddhist
Sit croass legged up a tree
While listenin tae aw the bird songs
Ah'll forget aboot ma flat screen TV

Weer a pony tail et the back o ma big bald heid
Contemplate geein up the booze
Walk aboot wi ma jammie boatums oan
N a pair o trainin shoes
Bend ma boady intae a circle
Yaisin a tae, ah'll scratch ahin ma lug
Play mind gemmes wi aw the animals
N freek oot ma paer wee dug

Ah want tae be a Buddhist
Weer rid, yella, n orange claise
Levitate inside ma big robes
Weer sandals wi sticky oot taes

Ah've goat a temple in ma bedroom
Where ah chant oot aw these songs
Interspersed wi silence
An the ringin oot o gongs
Ma belly's fu o lentils
Ma farts smell o figs
Ah've went richt back tae nature
Ah've even gave up the cigs

Yiv goat tae live in the moment
Mindfulness will set yi free
So if yi don’t believe me
Jist shut yir een, then yi’ll see

– J.V.

"The Bottle Said Canary Yellow"

....exclaimed big Dougie Thomson. It was March 1982 and things were looking a bit down for the boys, and girls, on the Fairlie and District Rangers supporters' bus, on their way to the "Old Firm" game in Glasgow.

John Grieg might have been a club legend, but as a Manager, let's be honest here – he was rank rotten. The team he had assembled consisted of such luminaries as Gregor Stevens, John "Polaris" McDonald and Davie McKinnon. About the best you could say for most of them was that they were "good triers" or "hard working pros".

This was all a far cry from 1972, when Scotland's biggest club had swept triumphantly through Europe with the likes of Colin Stein, Willie Johnston, Sandy Jardine and Greig himself, lifting the European Cup Winners Cup in Barcelona.

The Fairlie bus used to pick up other Rangers supporters at the Greenock shipyards in those days. The fans from Fairlie and Greenock got on well enough but you couldn't help noticing the differences between the country yokels from Ayrshire and the urbanites from Inverclyde.

Young Dougie was an example of that. On he comes at Greenock, a young punk. Black leather jacket with Joy Division graffitid on the back, skin tight tartan trousers and bum flap, five earrings in one ear, two in the other, and wait for it......... bright green, yes GREEN!!, sticky up Mohican hair.

Old Tam Williamson, President of the Fairlie Rangers club for 30 years, Boys Brigade Captain, Grandmaster Mason, Church of Scotland Elder and shopkeeper, looked like he was about to fall off his throne at the front of the bus.

"In the name o' Goad son, whit've ye done tae yer hair?". Dougie, who seemed to be genuinely distressed, looked at him, "ah don't know auld yin, it sayed canary yella oan the boattle".

– Fraser Falconer

Changing Me

I won't remember your name
But I'll remember your face
My short term is gone
But my long term's in place

I love to sing in the morning
And sing in the night
And I'll sing behind the till
When I'm feeling alright

I won't remember your name
But I'll remember your face
My short term is gone
But my long term's in place

Lots of things now have a different taste
All the things I used to like have gone to waste
From bacon rolls to garlic and sausages too
Do I really miss the things that I once knew?

I won't remember your name
But I'll remember your face
My short term is gone
But my long term's in place

– Katya Bisset

Mr Magnanimous

Some gym goers get sanctimonious
I try keep it harmonious, not acrimonious
with my sagacious Bruce Lee
doppelgänger acquaintance.

Results come from continuous practice
It helps that the gym is salubrious
commodious without parsimoniousness.

With Gary the gym worker's guidance
things don't get insipid or repetitious
or egregiously residually injurious
the secret's to keep it spontaneous.

– John Campbell

The Zoo

Down at the Zoo
You see wonderful things
Pandas on roller blades
Elephants on swings.

Giraffes on skateboards
A bear with a kite
Camels on ice skates
What a wonderful sight

A lion and a tiger
Are trying to tease
A large hippopotamus
On the flying trapeze

The day is now over
We leave with much sadness
But we'll come back again
For more animal madness

– Mike Gallagher

Cold Winter Paper

Now the ice on the paper have made me colder times
Now ice in my world it's freezing all over me
My own writing is out there need to catch make me feel warmer
Got the ice on the paper with the cold words that they send
And now don't make me feel warm
My river is now frozen over
I need to feel warmer with the words I send to my river
Learn the time to move the ice away
I now need warmth in words and make
the ice on paper to cry away
My own warm world it's now in
Stopped the ice to give me there winter freezer
I now melting the ice on my paper
My warm words walking on my paper make me feel the warmth

– Steven Walker

Down By The Seaside

I woke up after having been out all night with my mates one of them was/is getting married. I am absolutely sure, well to be honest that is I am ninety nine percent sure, that I went to bed in a bed; mattress, duvet, pillows and everything that a normal bed should have. Whatever I am lying on is far too low to the ground, reminds me of every jail I have been in. Tell me it is not a cell. I hate waking up when your belt has been removed in case when you are cosmically drunk you can still find a way to hang yourself; what usually happens is that your pants start to fall down and you fall down with them, hit the cell floor nose first. It's not very pleasant but it makes a belter of a noise.

Here I am on the low down bed. I open my eyes slowly anticipating the pain that shall follow. I open them all the way, close them, and do this a couple of times. No headache, in fact I feel pretty healthy.

I get up off the floor and look around my bedroom which is in fact my whole house, a circle about twelve feet in diameter, eight feet high and made from straw. There is nothing in it except the bed. I am naked apart from a loin-cloth. Not exactly Tarzan material.

There is a knock on the hut wall. What do I do?

- Are you okay? May I come in?
- Describe yourself?
- Sorry.
- Go on, paint me a picture.

- Okay. I am about head height and light green in colour. Will that do?
- Come on in then.

Sure enough, in comes a person. Head height and light green in colour. I'm taking this rather well.

- Where am I?
- Down by the seaside.
- Can I watch the ships sail by?
- The last occupier of The Hut said that as well. What does it mean?
- I have no idea any more. It didn't mean that much anyway. So I am down by the seaside. Can I get some food?
- There is some in The Hut. Go in, get washed, have something to eat and when you come back out we shall talk some more. My name is Light Green by the way.
- Matthew. Pleased to meet you Light green.

This is going much better than I expected it to go. I am definitely not back home with a wee front and back garden. I don't have a dog or guinea-pigs to feed. I am down by the seaside, the sea goes on forever, the temperature is warm, the atmosphere perhaps a bit too humid. A nice place to come to on holiday, but not one to wake up to after a night out.

When I enter The Hut, sure enough, the bed had gone. It had been replaced by a long table covered in fruit, cereal and fish, and a book. Whatever happened I was well on my way to “five a day”.

The book was a guide to the beach which was, well, a beach. The book said that was all that there was, it did go inland but if you were sensible you stayed on the beach. It had a population of 75 which was composed of the oldest person on the beach, everybody else, and The Oracle. Everybody who occupies The Hut must go and visit said Oracle to decide. This is where the book stops.

I finish reading the book and go back outside. Light Green is there skimming stones and is pretty good at it - they seem to go on forever. Also she seems to have gained considerable height. She hears me and turns round. Another thing strikes me as being strange: the beard.

- You’re staring you know.
- You’re taller and have a beard.
- I know. Light Green told me you were in The Hut reading about us.
- So what do I call you?
- Light Green.
- What are the other people who live here called?
- Light Green, apart from the oldest one who is called “Oldest Light Green” and the oracle who is called “The Oracle”.

Makes sense in a beachy kind of way.

- Do you want to go and see The Oracle now, or do a bit of sightseeing first?
- I think I shall get The Oracle over and done with. We're approaching cognitive overload at the moment.
- Funny you should say that. The last person from The Hut said that as well.
- Where are they now?
- They made their choice.

That helped me a great deal, told me everything yet explained nothing.

- I think I shall just go and see The Oracle.
- Follow the yellowed mud road till it stops. Knock on the door.

Sounds pretty straightforward, but I have a feeling that this is wishful thinking on my part. I start up the yellowed mud road. I have only gone a few steps when I realise I am singing a song I cannot remember and Light Green (with the beard) is no longer with me. It is really quite pleasant, I climb over the last sand dune and realise why no one strays off the beach. The sand gives way to boulders with steam pouring from deep fissures which constantly change. The sky is no longer blue, but some horrific brown colour with tomato skin clouds.

Suddenly this is not a nice place to be. The road goes on forever until, just like Light Green said it would, it stops.

In front of me is a cliff the width of the road. I peek round the corner of the cliff face, it is only an inch or two thick. Beyond the corner is nothing, well, nothing that makes any sense. I am looking at an audience of Light Greens, in a cinema, in a void, not unlike my local multiplex back home. They all have “do it” looks on their faces.

Quickly I turn come back from the edge, ignore what I have seen, and look at the cliff. There is a door, with a huge brass knocker in the shape of a face. It has been used too much and is stuck to it’s centre. I grab it and the face changes to one of “oh god not again”. I immediately leave it alone, and it sort of relaxes.

I get myself back together, grab it again, lift it up and drop it.

- Jesus I hate when people do that to me, the knocker says.
- But that‘s what you’re there for.
- So that means I can’t have feelings, god I hate you people.

A talking door knocker. A bell I could have coped with, but this ...

- Just hold on and I’ll get The Oracle for you. Don’t go away.
- As if!
- Pardon!
- Okay.

I stood waiting, looking back the way I came. It looked back. I ignored that and turned to face the door. The knocker had disappeared; only to be replaced by a bell. This I could handle.

- Press me baby.
- Am I going to feel bad about this?
- You could do.

I press the bell and almost immediately a voice I am sure I recognise from somewhere says - come in.

The door slides down into the ground, and I once again can see the audience. They have smiles on their faces, apart from Light Green who is knitting. Instantly they are replaced by a candle lit passage I hear the sound of elevator music.

- So what do you want?
- I am here to see The Oracle, Light Green sent me.
- So what do you want?
- Still don't know.
- Oh well, come in then, follow the steps till they stop. Someone shall meet you there.

The steps are steep and the colours continually change, on the wall, floor, and ceiling. Reminds me of an old Jack Nicholson movie. I reach the bottom of the stairs, and there's Janet from the corner chip shop.

- Not what you were expecting!
- What makes you say that?
- Well it's just that ... oh forget it.
- You haven't changed much.
- What brings you here?

Damn good question, something I never really considered. I don't think I'll consider it now either.

- Have no idea.
- How about yourself?
- No, can't say I think about it much either. Being The Oracle beats working in the chip shop though. Okay you are no longer where you were yesterday. This you know already, so you have two choices.
- What would those be?
- You can either go back down to the beach and be fed to the really vicious animals ...
- Not too keen on that what's the second one?
- You can go back down to the beach and fight Oldest Light Green. All you have to do is knock him to the ground.
- Is there a catch?
- Of course there is.
- Thought so. Okay, I'll take option two.
- Go back up the stairs, down the yellowed mud road, and back onto the beach. They shall be waiting for you there.

The walk back to the beach is much the same as the walk to The Oracle. The only difference is that when I get back, the beach is crowded with Light Greens. I walk onto the beach and they part. There is a circle of hard packed sand that was not there when I left, but so many things change here that it no longer bothers me. I go into the circle and am handed a huge deck brush. This bothers me. I look around, and sure enough Oldest Light Green is there dressed as a ship's captain. Things are getting scary now. He looks about a hundred and fifty years old, so I think to myself this should be easy. I shall just rush at him and knock him over using my weight.

We both go into the circle, me upright, he bent and crooked, me with the huge deck brush, him dressed as a captain.

My plan is simple. Run at him, knock him down, game over. I start my run then something unexpected but totally in keeping with everything that has happened to me so far happens, the beach moves. Actually it disappears from underneath me. I am falling through empty space when I remember the deck brush.

I swing it up over my head and it catches onto the edge of the beach. I look up in front of me. There they are, Light Greens and Oldest Light Green still on the beach. Look to the right, nothing. Look to the left, nothing. Look underneath, nothing. Look right above me, all the clouds have formed the short phrase "Wrong Choice".

Oldest Light Green walks up to the edge of the void and kicks the deck brush off the beach. As I am falling through nothingness and the beach disappears my last thought is "Janet, I was not expecting that".

I fall through space, my head points to the edge of the beach. 75 heads look down at me. Their heads slowly disappear one by one until there are only two left; Oldest Light Green and Janet The Oracle.

Janet tenderly leads Oldest back from the hole and gives me a sad little wave. Does she think I shall come back? Now I am left on my own in free fall it is actually a really nice feeling it's not cold, not warm, just right. When you fall they say your life flashes before you so here goes.

It starts with me waking up on the beach ... that's not fair I am more than one day old. I wake up on the beach follow the yellowed mud road talk to The Oracle and then end up tumbling through space (when I think about it it looks like a lift shaft, the sun is shining down and giving measurement).

The sun moves over the edge and my surroundings are now dark. Will I belly flop when I hit the bottom, head first, feet first?

A memory flits into my brain. It was of my first diving instructor. She said that once you are in the air you can make your body do anything, a back somersault followed by a twist into a forward somersault. A 360 degree vertical twist.

The sun reappears and I land feet first into strawberry jelly whereupon I lose consciousness.

– Neill Sloan

The Monklands Canal

When I was eight I almost drowned in the Monklands Canal. At that time, the canal ran from Easterhouse to Coatbridge. Now it's a motorway. The canal was very dirty. It was full of rats and rubbish. The water was supposed to be blue but it was black, with green fungus on top of it. As I was getting older they put in drains to start draining the canal for building the motorway. These drains gave me the fear. A wee fella who lived up the road from me died in those drains. When I hit the water it was the first thing I thought about.

I was with some of my friends and they were egging me on, trying to get me to swing over the Monklands on a rope. At the bottom the rope had a big frayed knot. You'd run and you'd jump onto the knot. It was a grey black rope, with a horrible smell, the smell of tar. It had seen a lot of people going on it, but it happened that I lost my grip and plunged into the Monklands. Within seconds my friends helped me out the water. They were older boys and pulled me right out. As soon as I was out I thought 'That's it!'. I was thinking about that wee boy, who hadn't been as lucky as I was. I never wanted to go back on the rope after that.

– Charlie McGoldrick

Memory Problems

In a world where everyone
had memory problems
everybody would be equal,
and understanding with each other.

They wouldn't laugh at others
or make fun of them, we might
still crack a joke about it, but
we'd all be in the same boat,
supporting each other, like a team.

Reminding and helping each other
with the bits we could remember.
Doing the things we like together.

– K.L.

Blocking My Light

I have been given the dark shadow in silence, my own voice is out there, I got to find and get free as I got trouble and don't belong here. It's burnt my mind and now I'm in a dry place and it's all over me and free my mind it's what I need. Now I don't want to sleep can't give myself a rest as I'm so lonely with the dark taking life off my needs. Stop the shadow tearing my life with the teeth. Now my whole new life is here with the light I meet the whisper in my mind next to my eyes with my belief and my future that belongs to me. I open up pull back the cover given by the shadow gives myself the prismacolor of a different place being my new life.

– Steven Walker

Exile From A Small Town

Nowadays I see myself as a kind of "exile" from my home town. Like many exiles I have mixed feelings about the place I have left.

My home town is a small town of about 11000 people. It is situated on the West Coast of Scotland, about 35 miles from Glasgow. My family on my Mother's side have lived in the town, or surrounding area, for several generations. I know this because one of my relatives looked into it and told the rest of us.

My Great grandfather was a farm Labourer on a farm about 2 miles to the North of the town. My Grandfather was the tenant farmer of the same farm. In the 1980's I worked there myself in Summer and Winter school holidays. It was backbreaking work, bringing in hay and neeps, but I loved it just the same. The hard work was compensated by the superb views from the farm out across the firth of Clyde to the Cumbraes, Arran, Bute and the Argyll hills. On a dark winter's evening, while loading neeps for cattle feed, I could look far out across the sea and see the slow rhythmic flashing of the Toward lighthouse. For some reason I always found this comforting.

I have always loved the physical aspects of the old town and the area in general. The sea in all its moods and colours - blue and sparkling on a long, bright Summer's day, grey, sullen and choppy or ferocious and wild on a Stormy winter's day. I love all of these; they make you feel close to nature. Many times I walked my dog along the promenade after a storm, weaving in-between the debris – thousands of stones and bits of wood thrown up from the angry spume. It gave me a sense of contentment and exhilaration at the same time.

Then there are the towering green hills which rise up behind the town. These create a natural barrier which gives the town its unique sense of place. I have roamed all over these hills since I was young just for the exercise and the superb views.

So my identity is tied up with the town whether I like it or not, but there's another twist in this tale because up to the age of seven years old I lived abroad, in the Gulf, where my Father had a job in the oil industry.

When we, came back to live in Scotland, I was a bit of a stranger, even in this town where my family was so deeply rooted. The weather also took a bit of getting used to after the sunshine of the Gulf!

I learned the hard way that there was a pecking order, rigidly enforced, in this small town. Your place in the pecking order had little to do with individual merit and instead depended on things like family status and what part of town you lived in. The latter had two aspects to it i.e. there was a wealth pecking order relating to snobbishness in that the wealthier part of town was higher up the pecking order. However there was also, in direct contrast to the other pecking order, another, which was that the rougher part of town you came from, the more "street cred" and fighting ability you were deemed to have. So someone brought up in a rougher area could be expected to have "hard man" status over someone who wasn't just by dint of where they lived.

I seemed to struggle to come to terms with this new reality. In my new primary school I was in trouble many times with teachers as I rubbed up against other people's ideas of who I was. I didn't realise it at the time, but I can see now that I was challenging these pecking orders in my own way.

Needless to say this didn't always end happily for me, but I was stubborn and refused to be pushed off my own path and let others define me. In the home we had family problems with alcohol and other related issues. This led to more unhappiness for me with trying to protect my young brother from the worst of these.

Despite these problems, I still loved the town at that time, the sea, the hills, and the sense of community. However there weren't a lot of job opportunities there in the 1980's so I left to go and live in London when I was 19. I came back after a year, and then left again at 22 to be a student on a 3 year College course in Glasgow. By the time I was 24 I had been away for nearly three years. I had enjoyed living in the City but hadn't wanted to live there for the rest of my life. I liked the idea of living in a small town that also had easy access to the city, so I went back home again.

But my love for the town was about to come under severe challenge. One Saturday night, shortly after moving back, I went out for a few drinks with some pals. We decided to finish the night off with a curry. When we got to the local Indian restaurant we joined a queue for a table. Some well known troublemakers came in and walked to the front of the queue. Me and my friends were unhappy about this queue jumping and so decided to complain to the manager.

This in turn enraged the thugs and they turned on us, a huge punch up broke out. It was broken up by kitchen staff and the troublemakers were pushed out the restaurant. When it looked like it had all died down, me and one of my pals who lived in the same direction as me, started walking home.

On our way, we heard a noise from behind, we turned round and the three thugs were right behind us. As I turned round, one of them smashed a rock into my head just on the frontal lobe on my left side causing my skull to fracture. My head exploded with blood and my left eye closed immediately and blood was pouring into the other leaving me "blinded". My first instincts were to get out the way as quickly as possible and get help for my mate. As the attackers set about my mate, I staggered onto the road where a police car was passing just at that moment. The thugs were arrested and me and my mate were rushed to hospital. The three thugs were all subsequently charged and convicted of serious assault, two of them were jailed.

Needless to say, an injury like that resulted in some serious problems for me. As well as commonplace head injury symptoms, I plunged into severe depression. I started to drink and smoke very heavily as symptoms of Post Traumatic Stress Disorder (PTSD) overtook me. I had a long term girlfriend but the relationship broke up under the strain. I became "hypervigilant" - a form of paranoia – fearing that I was about to be attacked again at any moment. My paranoia wasn't entirely irrational as I had received several threats before and after the trial of the attackers (This just made me more determined to do my duty as a witness).

My state of mental health spiralled downwards until eventually I just closed down emotionally and withdrew deeper and deeper into myself. I stayed in this state, living in my parents' house and hardly going out, for about 3 years. I was getting slowly better, but was still a long way from a complete recovery when I was offered a job in a place I had worked before (a residential outdoor Sports centre on the outskirts of the town). I knew I wasn't really ready for it, but I was under increasing pressure from my parents to leave the house. It was understandable in a way, they weren't getting any younger. I took the job and a few weeks later my Father told me he wanted me out the house for good.

I moved into a small room in the Outdoor Centre and stopped speaking to my parents. I was able to do the job with a bit of difficulty – because of memory and concentration problems I developed my own system of writing everything I had to do down on A4 paper at the start of each shift. I would then cross these off as the shift wore on, once I'd completed the task. I was doing this for 2 years and everything seemed ok.

However, a new line manager was put in charge of me and she was unsympathetic to my problems. Tensions increased between us when I heard she was ridiculing my problems and making fun of me having to write everything down. I complained to the overall Manager about this but he took her side. After this, the harassment got worse, not just from the line manager but with the Manager and his Assistant Manager joining in as well.

Eventually I had no other option but to take my case to the Union. They represented me well at the subsequent internal tribunal and we won a walkover victory as my complaint was upheld. All the Management team were found guilty of workplace harassment. I opted to leave the job and was awarded several thousand pounds in a settlement. By this time I had had enough of the town.

I moved back to Glasgow, at first sleeping on a friend's floor before getting a rented flat. I have now lived in Glasgow for 16 years since then, and this has challenged my identity in relation to the town. I have honestly tried to just forget the place completely, in order to "move on", but I have found that hard to do. I have spoken to and read about people who have been able to just start a new life elsewhere and put the past behind them, but I just can't seem to do it.

Over the years, my Father has died and my young brother also passed away. So there is only me and my Mother left. I made up with her a few years back and I now go back to the town to visit her every 2-3 weeks. When I go back, I always take a walk along the promenade from the pier along to the boating pond at the north end of the prom.

I have sometimes stood there on a dark, winter's night wondering about all these things: Why can't I let go of this place? Will I ever come back to live here? Could I stand to give up my anonymity and subject myself to the pecking order again? Is there just too much emotional baggage for that to happen now? Is this my home anymore?

I stand there pondering all these questions and I look out and see the timeless, rhythmic flashing of the old Toward lighthouse on the cold Winter's night, a guiding light to those sailing alone on the dark rolling sea.

– Angus Gunn

A Recollection

I don't know what he enjoyed the most.
Was it the smoking of the pipe
or was it the preparation of the pipe?

He certainly spent a long time preparing his pipe. As a child watching him I thought it a very complicated process. But hypnotising. St Bruno was the brand of tobacco he smoked and the matches were Scottish Bluebell.

I loved watching my Grampa make up his pipe. I loved watching the flame from the match be drawn downwards into the pipe and lighting the tobacco.

I remember the ever so distinctive smell of the pipe.
I remember my Grampa in his favourite seat beside the roaring coal fire. His faithful dog was at his feet as my Grampa read his newspaper and smoked his pipe.

Always remembered.

My Grampa, his dog and his pipe.

– Pandora

Genesis

Poetry is like giving birth.
This is not true. Delivery
slides on paper to meet you.

Flinging itself out like the sound
of a single kiss. Is not hard.
But incubation always is.

– Bob Gray

Commodities

Gold and silver, oil and gas
All these things will come to pass
Oil and gas, silver and gold
Lives are bought and lives are sold
Gas and gold, oil and silver
Rob and steal and pinch and pilfer
Gold and gas, silver and oil
Wreck and ruin, burn and spoil

– David Thomson

Where Dae Yi Steigh Noo?

Look this is very important
As I've said many times
We were economical with the truth
With expenses and fines

Ah ken, that's wheigh ah'm askin yi
Yir reputations stick lik glue
The patsies hiv aw bin cote
So where dae yi steigh noo?

Wiz it you
That goat yir moat cleaned
An yir wee hoose fur the ducks
Pits yir inheritance money abroad
Or avoids peighin aw yir tax
Hauf peighed yir cleaner
An wiz greedy tae the max?

I think my first owned house is now my third
And my second is now my first
Give me that to drink
I've got a terrible thirst

You'll need to ask my secretary
That'll be my son, daughter or wife
I don't like your attitude, waging wars
In the name of you people has been my life.

– J.V.

Burns The Brush Hand

Painting submarines
In Rosyth. Eight coats of primer
You got on with it

Painting pylons
I was the man in the middle
Hands wrapped in tape

Painting gas tanks
You work systematically
You work hard

– John Burns

Big Sister, Little Sister

I think it must be classic big sister, little sister behaviour.

I recognise so many things in my wee nieces that I remember from how we were when we were growing up. That is, me and my little sister.

Best friends one minute.
Falling out the next.
Wanting the exact same of everything
- shoes, jackets, keyrings, colouring books, stickers and so on

When I was reminded of something that I did I couldn't help but laugh. I was told that when we were out walking our dog one day I got stuck in the mud. When I stepped out of the mud I'd left my brand new wellies behind. Then I shouted at my little sister, "why did you make me do that?". She was ages away from me so it couldn't possibly have been her fault. My selective memory remembers everything except blaming my sister. When we got home we were best friends playing our favourite game together.

One minute my nieces are best friends. They want to sit on the same seat together or play on the swing together. But the next they are in a bad mood with one another for a really minor reason.

We fought together when we were little and were best friends as well. History is repeating itself. When I watch my nieces play I laugh sometimes because it's us all over again and it brings back memories.

I hope they appreciate each other as I do my little sister.

– Pandora

Meaning

Never stopped the life it made the meaning
I had my own made engine
Drive the distance for me to live
The direction I gave I don't wait to see
Never stop before I start
Broke to the outside and stopped
Walked, tripped up, my hope was dead
I was waiting for something else
Can't see my feelings anymore
Crawl to start on the new
It's so out of meaning to me inside
Rip me make to need
Hungry so hard to get
No more dream as they want me to go

– Steven Walker

Misanthrope

'I condemn everybody' – Scottish Politician

I condemn the Tories,
I condemn the Nats.
I deny heliocentricity,
I deny the world is flat.

I condemn television,
I condemn social media.
My bin is full of ripped up tabloids,
I'm hatching a plot against wikipedia.

I condemn consanguinity,
I condemn the hermit in his cell.
One's concerned with your bloody family,
the other with himself.

I condemn wisdom,
I condemn the empty head.
I deny any fruitfulness
in the leaders or the led

I condemn the world,
all ignorance and knowing.
I recommend nothing,
I condemn this poem.

– Bob Gray

The Sage

As I put pen to page
To vent my rage
Or to make a rhyme or two
I feel like a sage
From some distant age
Who never had a clue

– David Thomson

Clatty Pats

In 1984 I made my first visit to Cleopatra's or Clatty Pats as it was affectionately known, but it certainly would not be my last. My social life had been the same for a few years, split between Partick and the City Centre.

In the City Centre we usually went to where we thought was trendy and in those days it was Pythogoras, Maxwell Plums and the dancing in the Cardinal Folly.

In Partick my regular haunts included The Quarter Gill, Chequers, The Parallel Bars and for the dancing it was faithful Cinders which, being honest, was getting old and tired and losing its appeal. With Cinders losing its magic I tried another West End dancing establishment for the first time, on Saturday 2nd of May 1984.

Over the next few years Clatty Pats almost became a weekend ritual. After the pubs closed we would go and dance the night away.

The main hall entrance had a large wooden dance floor and a small sitting area. The other large bar was nice and had a lot of standing room. The bar was a comfortable space to hang around in, and it had a lot of matt black shelves for your glass to sit on, mirrors and fancy white and black walls, and a lovely red carpet.

The friendly, informal atmosphere ensured that beginners and visitors mixed easily and had a nice drink together. The bar was excellent with a wide choice of drinks.

We really liked Cleopatra's and met a lot of new people our age. Most Friday and Saturday nights we would dance the night away and make friends. It was not long until we were part of the weekend crowd. We would always congregate in the same part of Clatty Pats.

At that time I was living with my parents in Scotstoun, so I was glad when, in the early part of 1985, the housing association in Patrick contacted me to say I had got my own house. It was everything I wanted. It was bang in the middle of Patrick on Dowanhill Street. If you mentioned you stayed in Dowanhill to a taxi driver they'd think you stayed in the big, expensive houses up top, so you had to explain it was the housing association flats at the bottom or the meter would go up!

It's hard to explain how great it felt having a place of my own. It was brand new, an old tenement building that had been done up. It was a good size for one person – one bedroom, a kitchen, bathroom and a living room.

Everything was white or white wood, the walls, the ceilings, the floors, and all the rooms were empty. You could hear the subway trains stopping on their way through Patrick Cross (now Kelvinhall), even though the flat was on the third floor. The guy below me stayed by himself, and you could hear his radio through the floor in the evenings.

I officially got the keys on the 19th of February 1985 and spent most days down cleaning my new flat and getting furniture delivered in readiness for moving in.
There was, however, one small downside to getting my own place – I had to buy furniture for it. I could have curtailed my social life but that would've been too much of a sacrifice. So my beloved green Datsun Sunny car had to be sold.

I wanted a shower in the bathroom and it tiled, a red kitchen, which was the colour of the moment (although I think it's ugly now) Being 25 you buy a lot of rubbish as you only think about colours, I want red and white pots, and plates for kitchen, red cups, bread bin etc. Paint the doors on the kitchen units, they are green and I don't want that get red. I was red blind!

My living room white woodchip wallpaper, can paint that grey and get a nice grey carpet, new grey sofa. Lovely young girls house. Let's have a party and get friends up to see it.

I had moved up in the world and got away from the clutches of Mum and Dad, although both of them were great with me and helped me enormously with their work and also their financial help. The big day I had always dreamed about arrived Sunday the 17th of March 1985.

I can't explain how great it felt having a place of my own. After years of thinking and dreaming it was now reality.

A few drinks in the house with Terry on a Friday and Saturday night then we would go to cosmopolitan and trendy Byres road, places like Finlay's and Bonham's then end up in Cleopatra's

We really liked Cleopatra's and met a lot of nice people. Most Friday and Saturday nights Calum and his friends would be there. I had first met Calum a few years back and I really liked him. Calum was a friendly boy and he had a lot of friends. So it was not long until we were part of their crowd. We would always congregate in the same part of Clatty Pats then go back to my flat.

I suppose I had a crush on Calum and when I went to a Fortune teller, shortly afterwards, that crush became stronger.

The fortune teller told me I would marry at 26 and my husband's name would be Calum and we would have three children and live happy ever after. That convinced me it was only a matter of time before myself and Calum were a couple.

I met Calum and the rest of the crowd a few Friday nights afterward but never paid any attention when he stopped turning up on the Saturday nights.

Terry worked beside Calum's brother's girlfriend and they were getting married in September and I thought he would ask me to partner him. But no invitation came, However, I was still able to attend as Terry had an evening reception invite and I went as her partner.

To be honest the only reason I went to the wedding was to see Calum and likewise the main reason Terry was going was to see Gordy who she had lumbered previously and still fancied.

Calum was looking good all dressed up but my heart sand to the pit of my stomach when I noticed this girl constantly at his side and people looking at a new shiny engagement ring.

Yes, he had got engaged to someone else. Didn't he know he had the wrong girl?

I just wanted to go home but didn't feel like being on my own. You would think I was a daft teenager but I had always dreamt of marrying and having kids and convinced it would be with Calum. I should never had believed that stupid fortune Teller.

Despite having my fortune told the previous year I was not deterred and decided to arrange another visit from another fortune teller just before Christmas. So a crowd of girls gathered at my place and fortune teller informed us all of what lay ahead. She told me I would live in or near Anniesland sometime in my life. This is close to where I live now.

– Anne-Marie Ure

Restaurant Rap

I like eating out
I like getting about
And the Curry Shop
It gets my shout
Every Wednesday,
Down the Lane
I know what I want
It's always the same
Haggis Pakora Chasni King Prawn
I could eat that grub from
Dusk till dawn
Over 10 years now, it's my second hame,
My picture was up on the "wall of fame"

For a change I go to
The Italian Place
Three times a week,
I'm a well kent face
I know what I want,
It's always the same
Mushroom risotto is the name of the game
They make my risotto the way I like
All other risottos can take a hike!

– Katya Bisset

Why Climb Mountains

My sense of achievement was immense.

I knew it was going to be difficult but I enjoyed the preparation. I had bought the Ordnance Survey map and had studied it carefully. From the contours on the map I was able to plan a route. I have been fascinated by maps since childhood. We learned a bit about them at school and also something about geology, the ice age and how the mountains were formed.

I planned to lead the walking group up Beinn Ime, then down to a bealach and up Beinn Narnain, then down to Arrochar for the bus home. Phew! Could we do it? It could be awkward with public transport, but not impossible. There was no official bus stop at our starting point so I would have to ask the driver specially to drop us off at Butterbridge, dead noticeable from the wee hump-backed bridge. The bus home might cause a problem because we would have to be down by 7pm. There was only one bus back to Glasgow.

I did a recce of the walk with my father. We worked out the compass bearings between various points. This would mean we could follow them if the visibility was low on the day with the group. I figured that when we were at the top of each mountain we would know. I had planned a low-level alternative if the weather was really bad but as it happened it was a glorious day.

The enthusiasm for this walk was enormous. There were too many people to comfortably lead by myself so I asked for a couple of volunteers to help me.

The walk was a fantastic success. Well in advance people had been emailed information about the walk including advice about what clothes to wear. That meant to wear sturdy walking boots, comfortable clothes (not jeans) and to bring waterproofs. Also to bring plenty of food and water and to make sure they were physically fit enough. I had a first aid kit, survival blanket and whistle for emergencies and the map and compass. Today's walk leaders probably have a GPS (Global Positioning System), but I like the old fashioned way. Using a map and compass to navigate worked well, though on the actual day the sky was so clear that I didn't really need it. It's always good to be able to show people the route on the map.

We first headed up the grassy slopes of Beinn Ime. We were a colourful group of people. The different purples, reds, blues, greens and yellows of our waterproof jackets and rucksacks. There was a bit of a path but it was not always very obvious. It was wet underfoot at times as small burns flowed down the hillside. We reached the top of Beinn Ime and had a snack but did not stay for long because time was not on our side.

Most of the rest of the walk was dirt track with a bit of loose scree. We struggled in places. At some points it was really hard-going and we had to watch where we put our feet every step of the way. This was near the top of Beinn Narnain where there are huge boulders. Here it helped to use my hands to steady myself as I found my way. Others had no problems and like mountain goats stepped nimbly over these boulders. It was physically tiring and mentally exhausting. We carried on regardless. The summit was our goal. The view and achievement our reward.

It was extremely windy nearing the top of Beinn Narnain. We'd warmed up on the way, taking off layers of clothes. These layers went back on at the top because we cooled down really quickly when we stopped.

As walk leader I had become slightly stressed because one member of our group was quite a bit slower than the others, the group was large and I didn't like how spread out we'd become. I was grateful to the volunteer leaders. I stayed with the slow person, silently cursing him that if we ended up spending a night in Arrochar then he would be paying for the hotel! I didn't need to worry because with a bit of encouragement we ended up making the bus home. Thank goodness.

The enormity of the view from the top was absorbing. I stood there for ages taking it all in. A complete circle of panoramic view. The sky was blue, not a cloud to be seen. I looked at the mountains and at the map and tried to work out which was which. I added a rock to the cairn, a pile of stones that people can add to when they reach it. The stress of the busy city left me entirely. I felt at peace. My sense of accomplishment fulfilled. A person can become addicted to this feeling I think and want to feel it again and again.

Maybe there is some truth in the saying 'no pain, no gain'

– Pandora

The Dragon Trees

When the wind blows
The Dragon Trees wake,
Their heads start to nod
Their wings start to shake.

The tree soldiers stand there
Guarding their lair,
Tending the leaves
That blow in the air.

But when winter comes
With its gales and the cold,
The Dragon Trees slumber
Their leaves turn to gold.

When the leaves start to fall
On the Earth and the Stones,
The tree soldiers sleep
They can see only bones.

Then much much later
The Earth starts to warm,
The buds start appearing
The Dragon Trees yawn.

– Mike Gallagher

My Reality

Some part moving slow and using the time to be sullen with a sunless sky full of dark clouds. Some part having the object of longing for great feelings of wanting to have something to express a wish for. Sometime feeling like without power or influence feeling doubt and uncertain about my impossible regrets. These things do happen remain in existence and can refer to space as well as time. There are things in a way that is accurate and true to life and things are reel to reach out and touch.

– Steven Walker

A Little Daily Death

In her long life she has been a wife,
a mother, a grandmother.

She has been a sister, of two sisters
and a brother.

A mother to three sons.
An aunt to many, a great aunt too.

For many years an infant teacher.
All children grown, many remember her.

Since the diagnosis
her recollection of all
grows less and less.

I await the day
she remembers none of these.
I call this the little daily death.

– Neill Sloan

Time Capsule

Sometimes I use mind googling discombobulating words.
For this time capsule I'll say it straight and simple.

For those in the future who have an ABI
Structure in your everyday drive,
Navigate your aspirations,
Time will bring acceptance,
Focus, will and impetus,
Get on with it, give it your best.

– John Campbell

Participation

Participation is the
freedom to join in and
do the things you enjoy.

To take part some people
need transport and support.
Living with a brain injury

or other long term conditions,
like memory problems, can
slow you down and stop

you taking part or understanding
what's going on. In a discussion
it can be hard to give your views
with all the talk talk talk and jargon.

– K.L.

Maister O Communication

Me, ma angels n ma subconscious
Met up fur an adventure yin sunny day
We aw felt comfortable wi each ither
Fae the word go, we goat oan famously
We packed up oor jaickets n meal deals
Tiptaid oor weigh through possible screams
Left the city o oor realities
N headed tae the seaside land o dreams
In oor minds we solved everyhin
Days n weeks flew bye, bit stood still
Oot in the country we could see clearer
Shimmerin in the distance wiz that hill
We didnae take that wrang turnin
Naw we kept oan gawin roon the bend
Up ower, n alang the shoogily brig
Thinkin, ah hope this day disnae end

The spirits hid came, via their train station
Staunin wi their aw knowin sunny disposition
Wi nae fear, negativity or trepidation
We came upon oor glorious destination
An stood ootside the hoose o celebration

Then it wiz oan tae the elephants graveyaird
Where we stood there gawkin, lik wee weans
Cause the ruins o a familiar auld pyramid
Stood in the middle o awe thae baines
Wi a big sigh o accomplishment
We daunert oan, wi ither things tae dae
Saw a moose, a hoarse n a fox
N nain o them ran away

We were met wi dolphin smiles n open erms
When we stepped intae the cloud o tranquillity
Where we felt safe, loved n secure
Where oor desires n wishes were met wi serenity
We wur encouraged intae the tap table
Drinks wur cairit oot tae the gairden o romance
Gien a guided tour wi the lovin spirit o beauty
N realised we hid bin gein a saikent chance

The soothsaying oracle appeared tae us
A smooth black maister o communication
We could hiv steighed n listened aw nicht
Tae this human richts inspiration
This mysterious n mythical figure
Whae wiz a sophisticated illustration
Filled me wi amazement, awe n wunner
N fired up ma creative imagination.

– J.V.

Brain

Brain you send thoughts all over me
letting my body know when I am tired
Brain you tell me when I am hungry
Brain you tell me to get help when
things are too fast or heavy.

Brain you are part of me
you are connected to my body
you even tell me to get help
with brain injury.

Headway you are part of me
you connect me with other people,
you understand memory problems,
you understand how we all feel,
with time you help us with recovery.

– Anne-Marie Ure

Recovery

I.

That Sunday morning I had a headache,
I asked my girlfriend if she'd make
me a Lemsip. She said aye alright,
went down and got the kettle boiling.

She came back up,
asked me my name.
I told her John Burns.
She asked my address.
I told her. She was a nurse,

she noticed something
was happening.
My mouth had collapsed
on one side.

She was going to phone
the doctor but instead
called the ambulance.
I can remember that
Sunday morning
as if it was yesterday.

The paramedics
carried me
down the stair
in a wheelchair,
the siren
was going
but I didn't hear it.

Seven weeks later,
I went to the butcher's
in Alloa, asked for
sausages. I realised
then that recovery
was going to take
a long time.

II.

The first thing I noticed
was that I was always starving.
In the hospital ward there was
an orderly who used to walk in
with porridge for us. The other guy in
the ward didn't want it, so I'd eat both.

Every day. For seven weeks.
Two bowls of porridges. Two breakfasts.
Two lunches. Two dinners.
When I came out I was fifteen stone.

When I was out I started going walking
again, watching Jeremy Kyle with a cup
of tea. Trying to get my brain around it.

Frustration wasn't there all the time,
but now and again it would come into
my head. I wasn't feeling fine, really.
I'd sleep when I came back from shopping.
The days were an uphill climb
with a splint on my right leg.

I had it there for six year
but, in terms of pain, it
was completely clear.
I couldn't feel anything.
Just the frustration.
Now and again.

III.

Recovery is still going on.
Once I get the muscle done
on my right foot it will be
a hundred times better.
Then the toughest times are over.

I'll have to get my arm done too.
It takes time. It feels like it takes
an eternity. The way to get through
is determination.

Last week, I left the house,
and after a ten minute walk
I reached the cycle track to Kirkintilloch.

There were runners on it, walkers,
everything. You meet a lot
of people on it. I passed the baths
on the way, then I knew I'd only got
a short distance left to the main street.

All that was on my mind was to
get there, get to my destination.
One foot in front of the other.
Inner determination.

– John Burns

No More Poetry

No more poetry
tonight. Bar's shut.
The CLOSED
sign should be up
in lights.

As Chargehand,
on behalf of the staff,
thank you
for your custom
and conversation.

We appreciate
your hard luck
stories, your stress,
timing and
intonation.

Be they wrapped in
villanelles,
sonnets,
epistles
to the missed

or a free form verse
like a song
forgetting its chorus.
We treasure them all.
Great and small.

And no,
though you have
never asked,
of course
they never bore us.

They could be
prescriptive,
descriptive,
condemnatory,
hateful

or about lambs
gambolling over
summer lawns,
stylistically
the horses

may have bolted
from the cart.
Mainly they're
about your
broken hearts.

But it is the art
of the good bartender
to be forever Stoic,
like Zeno the Greek
with glass and towel,

nodding sagely with
all poets whether
wild, lost or meek.
We don't say it aloud
but in our eyes

you can read,
yes, neglected friend
in this world so foul
we know
what it is you seek.

But alas,
time, once again,
ladies and
gentlemen,
has taken flight.

You've turned our
stones into hearts,
but we have a home
to go home to
tonight,

it's not only poets
who wish
the privilege
of solitude
or a new life,

always could have been,
should have been
a contender.
Many lose
the good fight.

Now I'll let the sink
drink your dregs
and dreams.
Slurp down
your lost

consonants
and vowels,
structures
and tricky
schemes.

When you leave,
I'll turn out
the light.
Goodnight.
Goodnight.

– Bob Gray